MEN IN UNIFORM

ADULT COLORING BOOK

M.G. ANTHONY

T0019525

A POST HILL PRESS BOOK
ISBN: 978-1-68261-131-9

Men in Uniform Adult Coloring Book
© 2016 by M.G. Anthony
All Rights Reserved

No part of this book may be reproduced, stored in a retrieval system, or transmitted by any means without the written permission of the author and publisher.

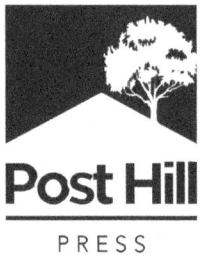

Post Hill Press
275 Madison Avenue, 14th Floor
New York, NY 10016
posthillpress.com

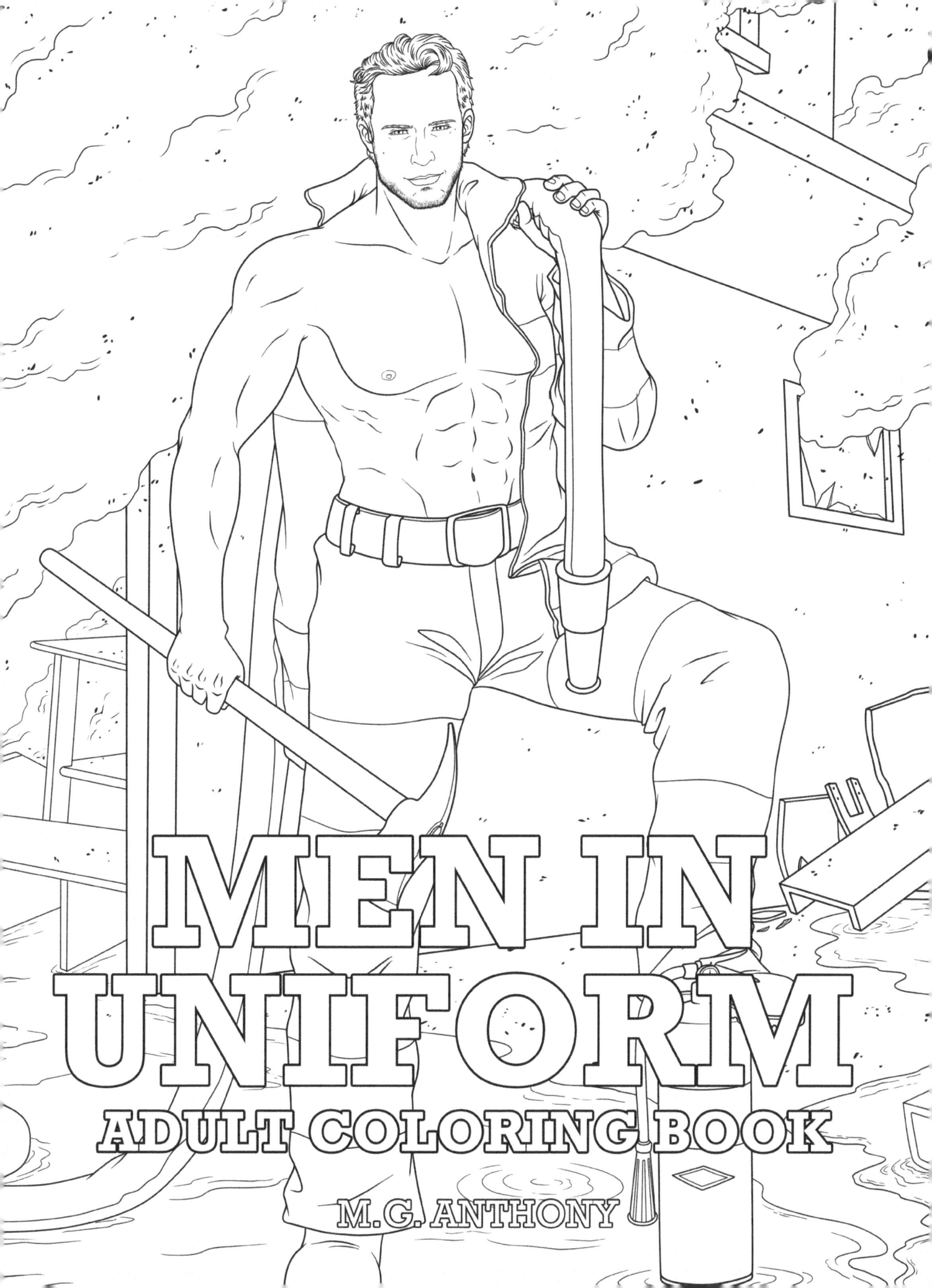

MEN IN UNIFORM

ADULT COLORING BOOK

M.G. ANTHONY

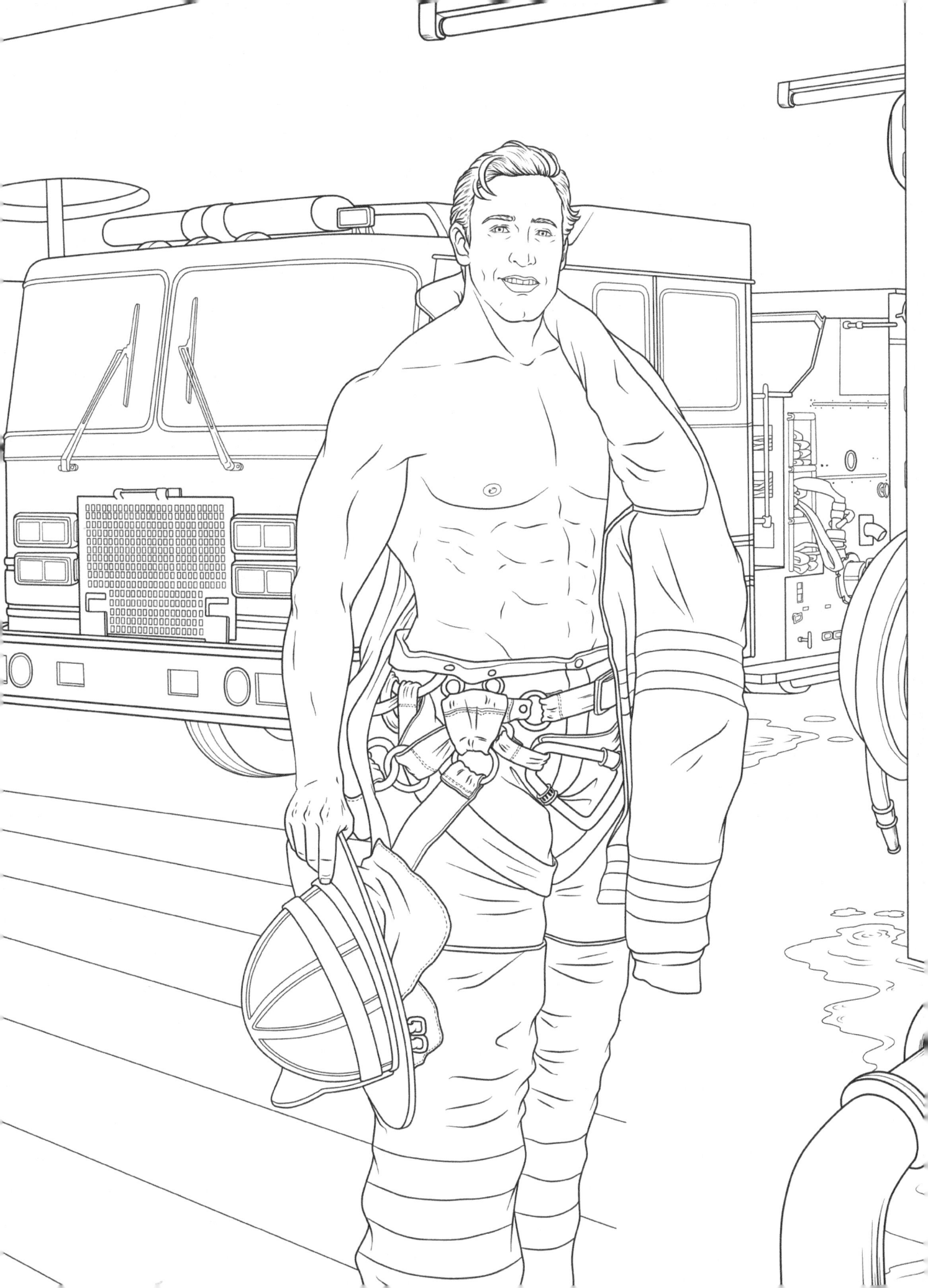

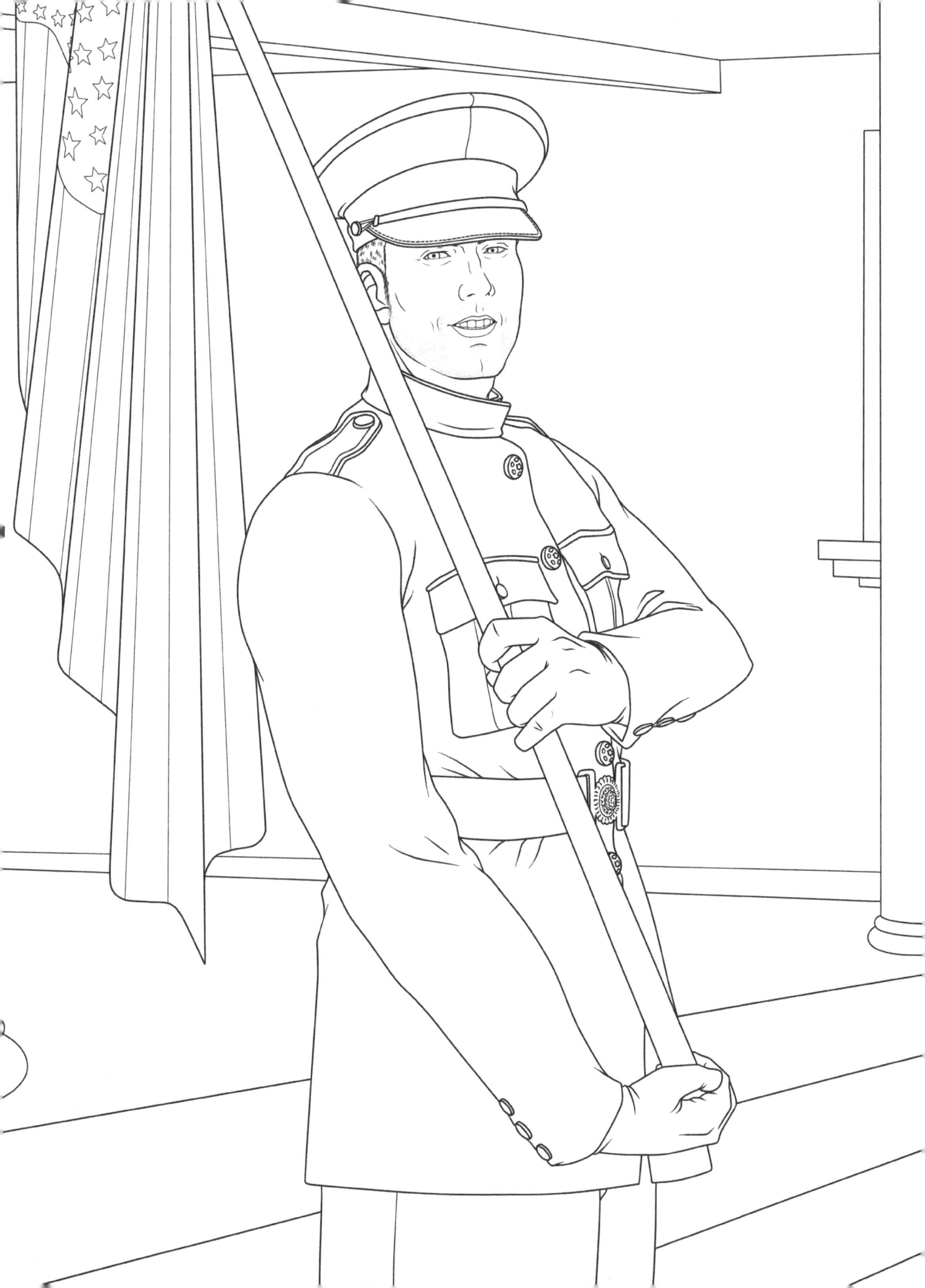

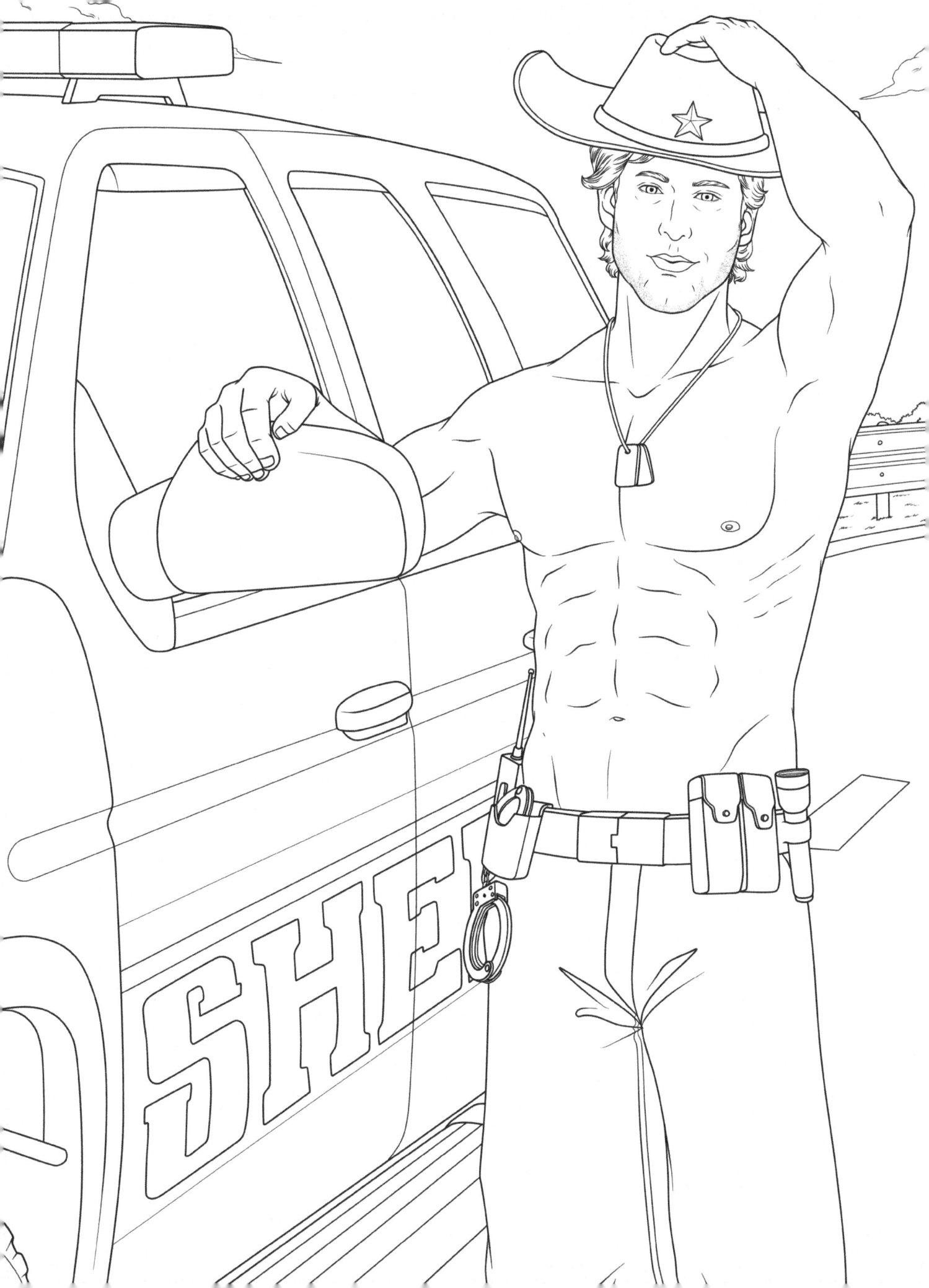
SHE

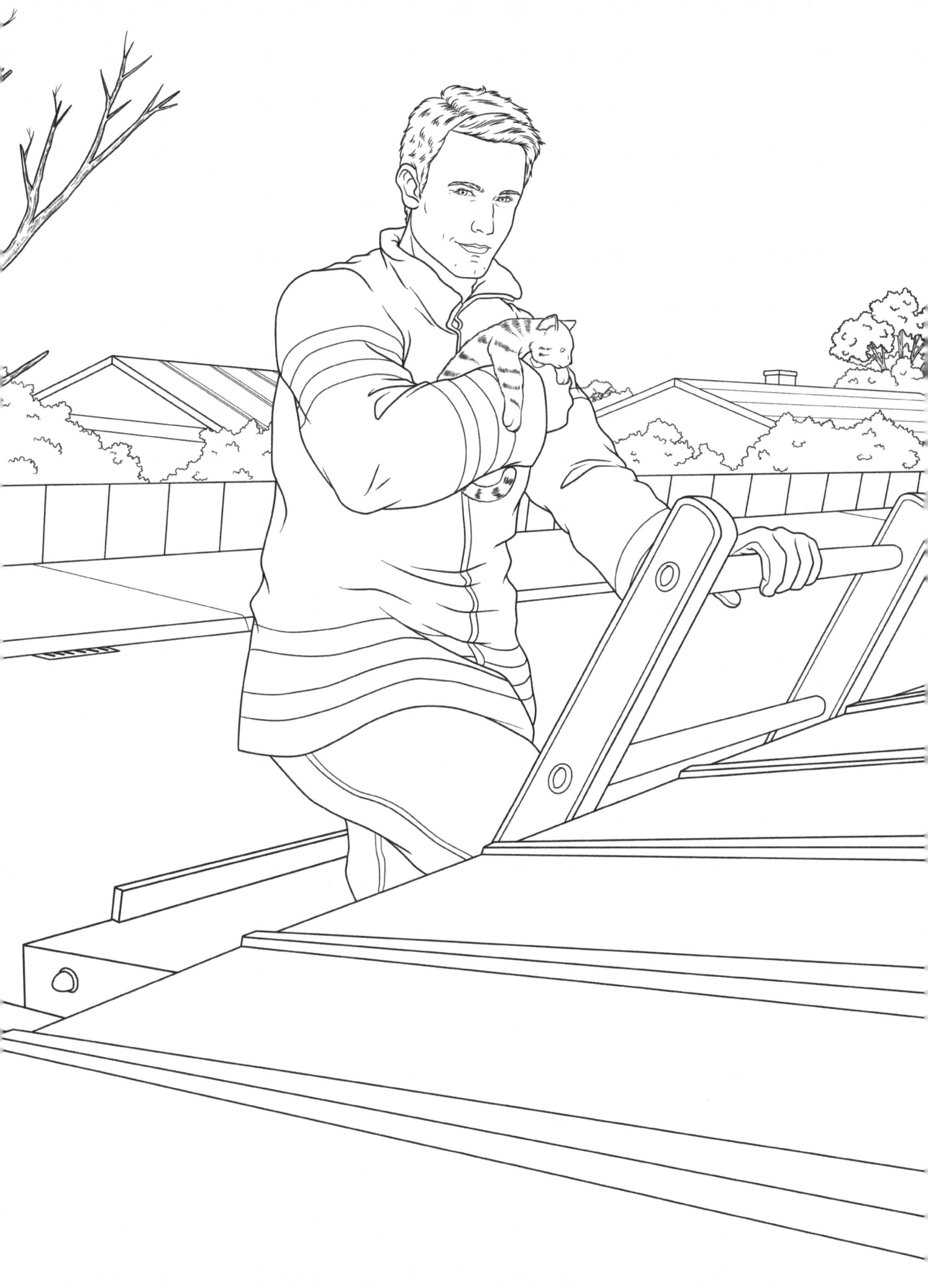

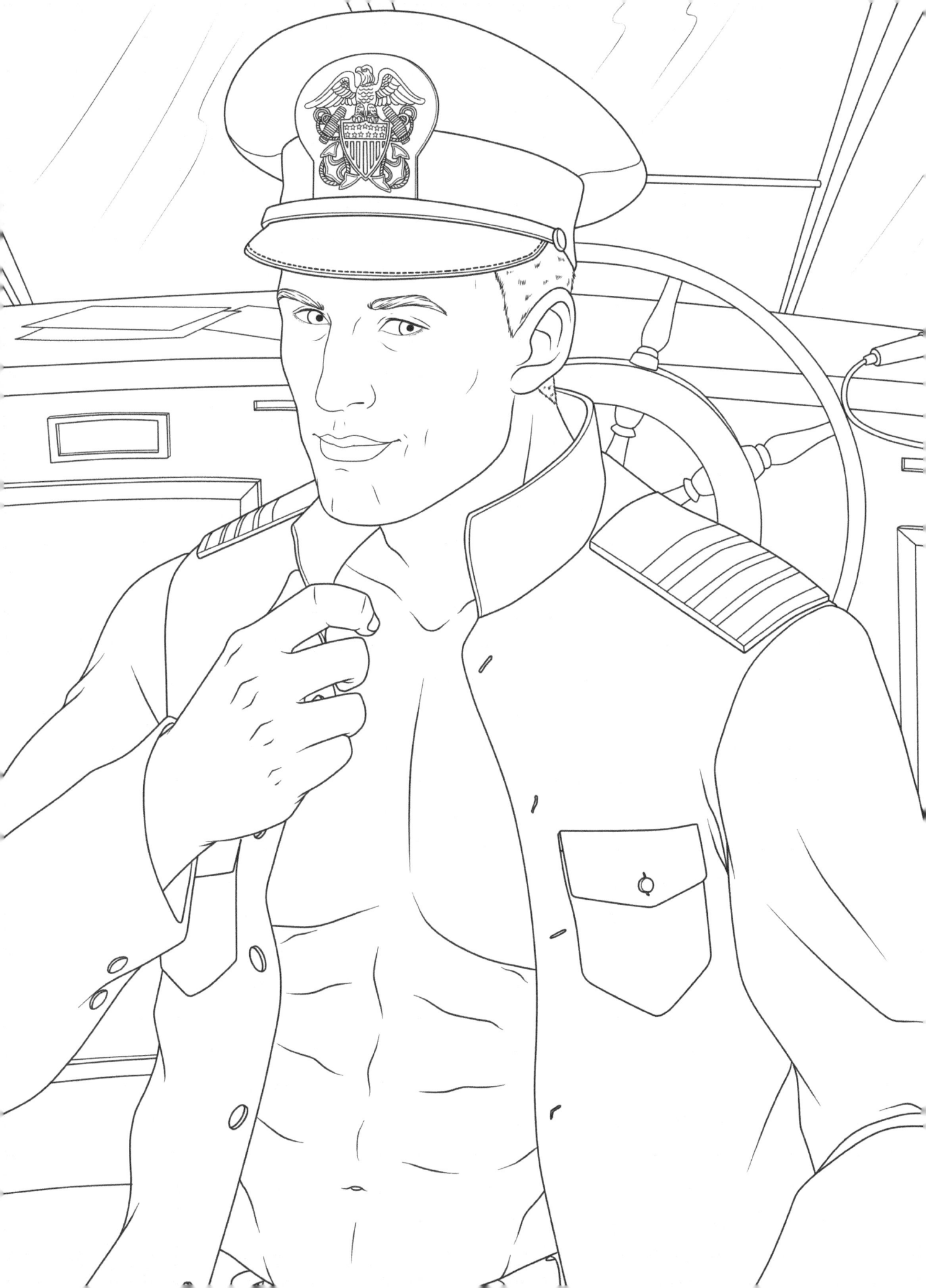

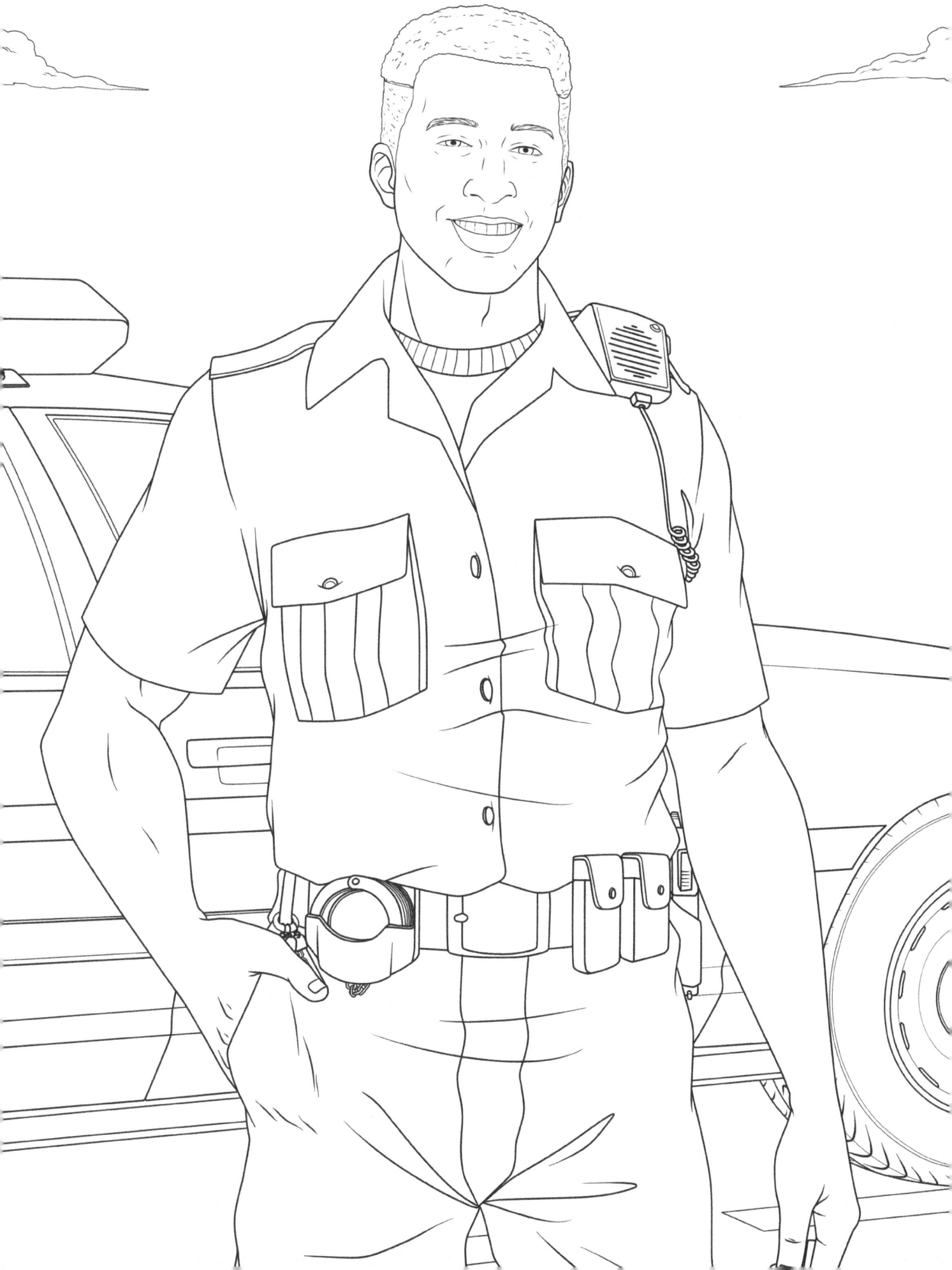

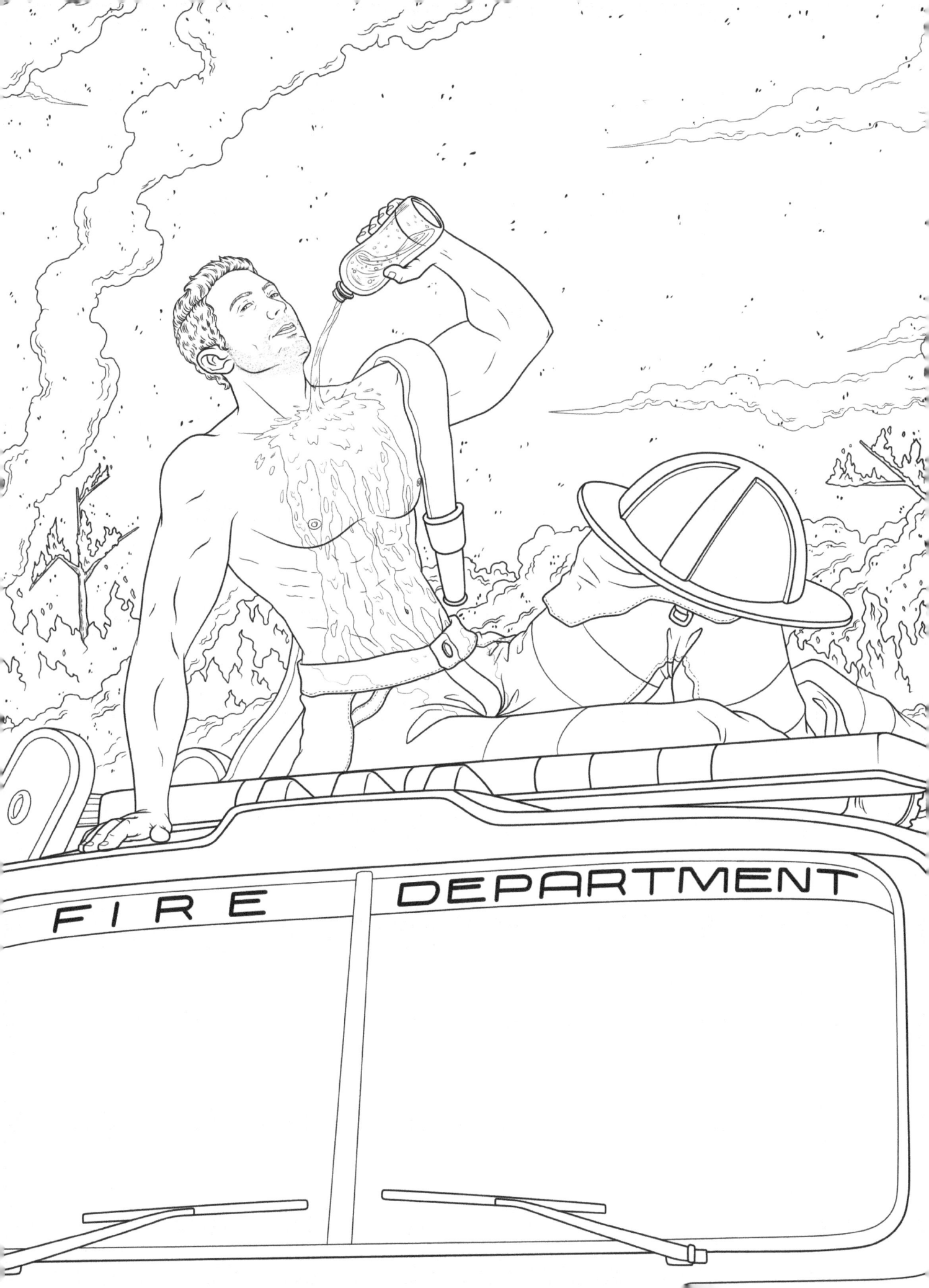
FIRE DEPARTMENT

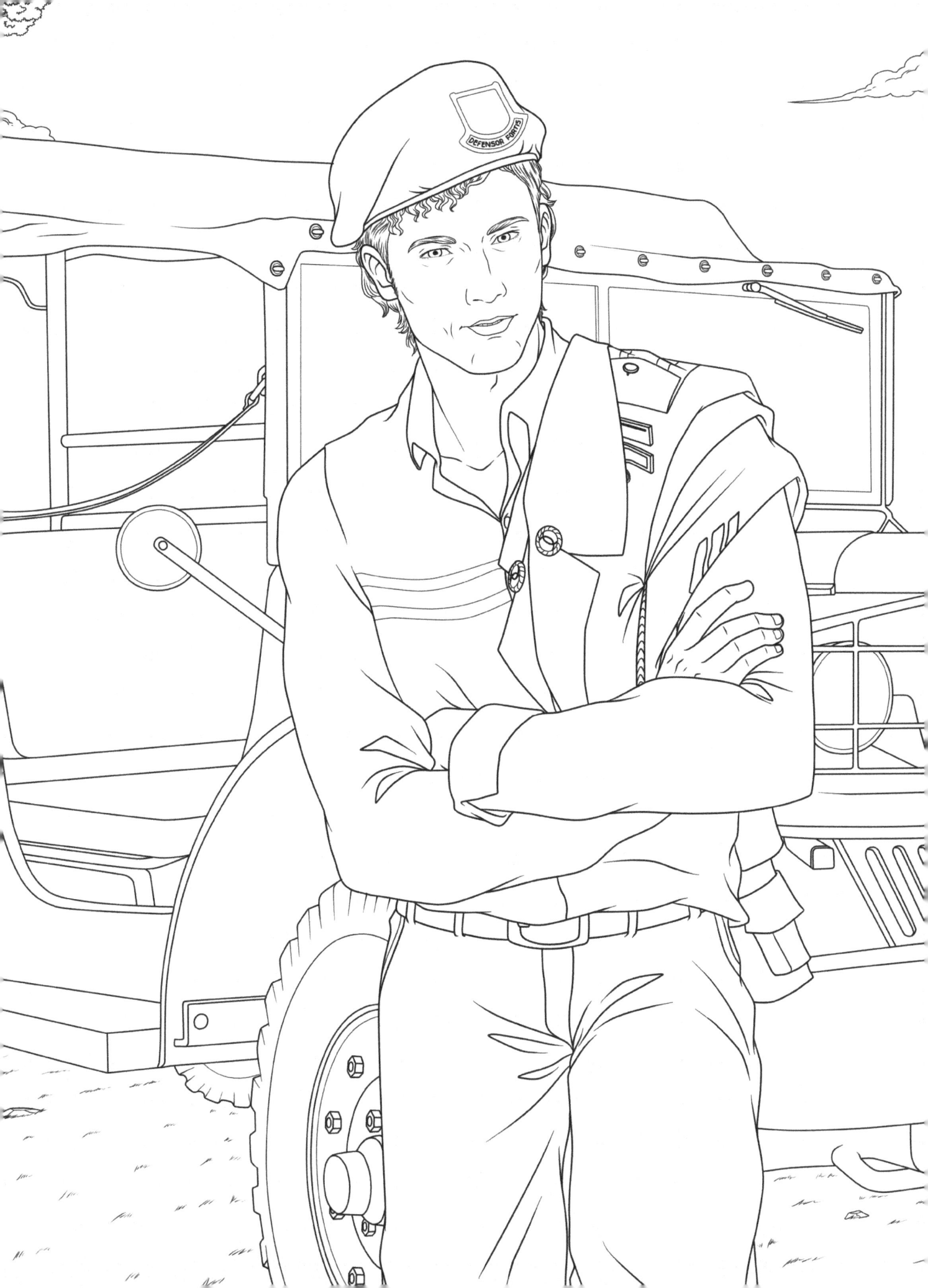
DEFENSOR FORTIS

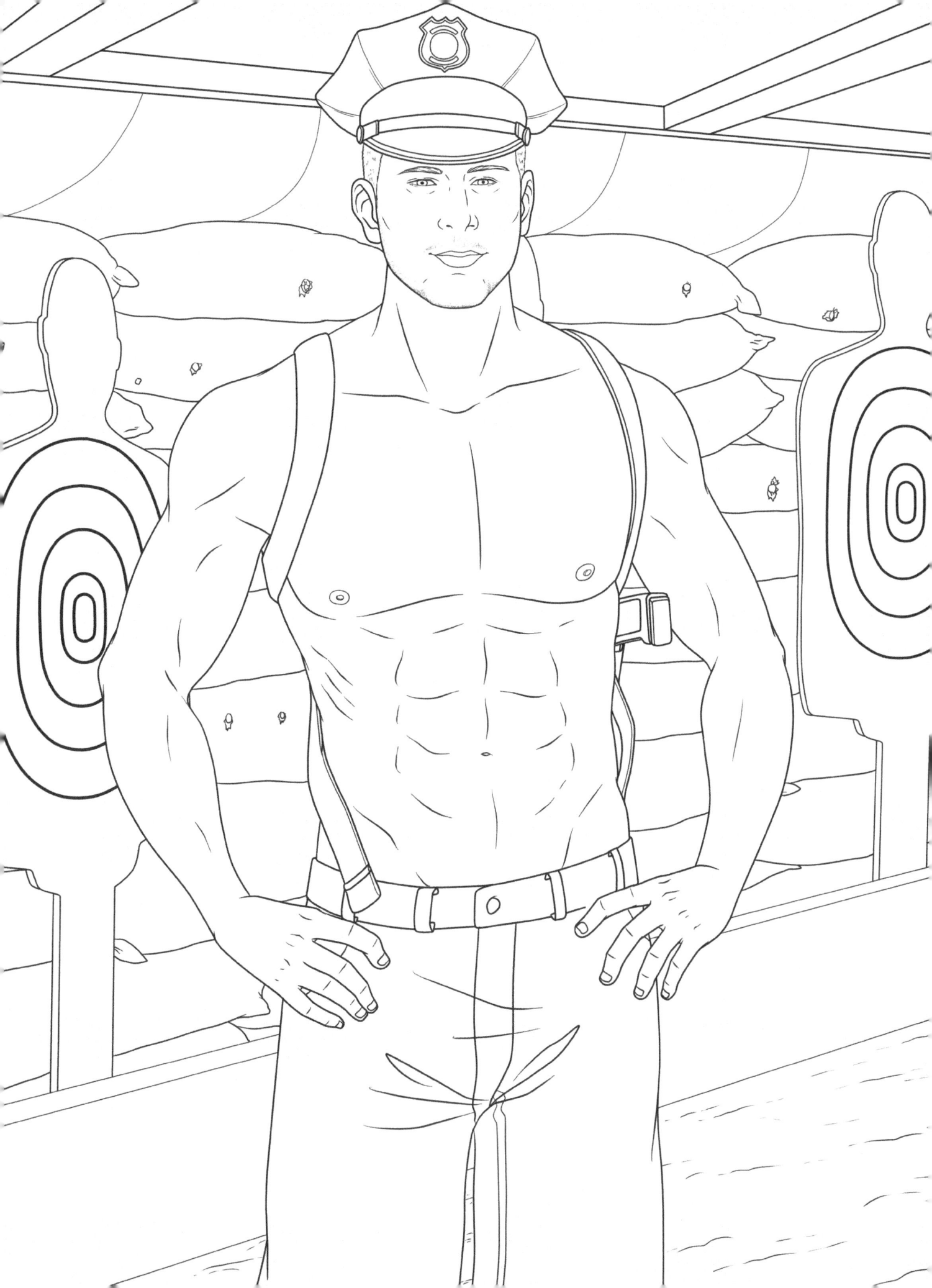

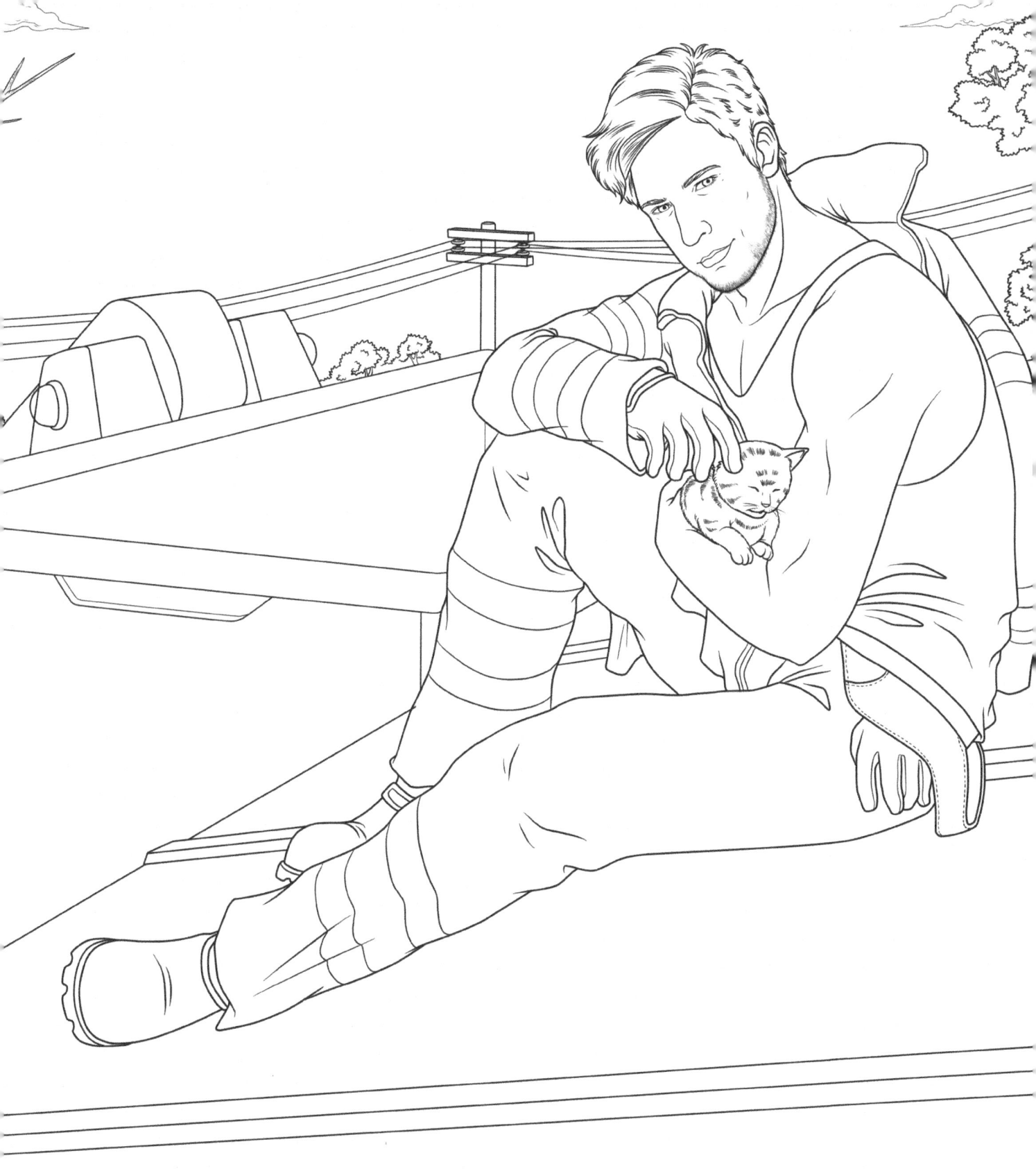

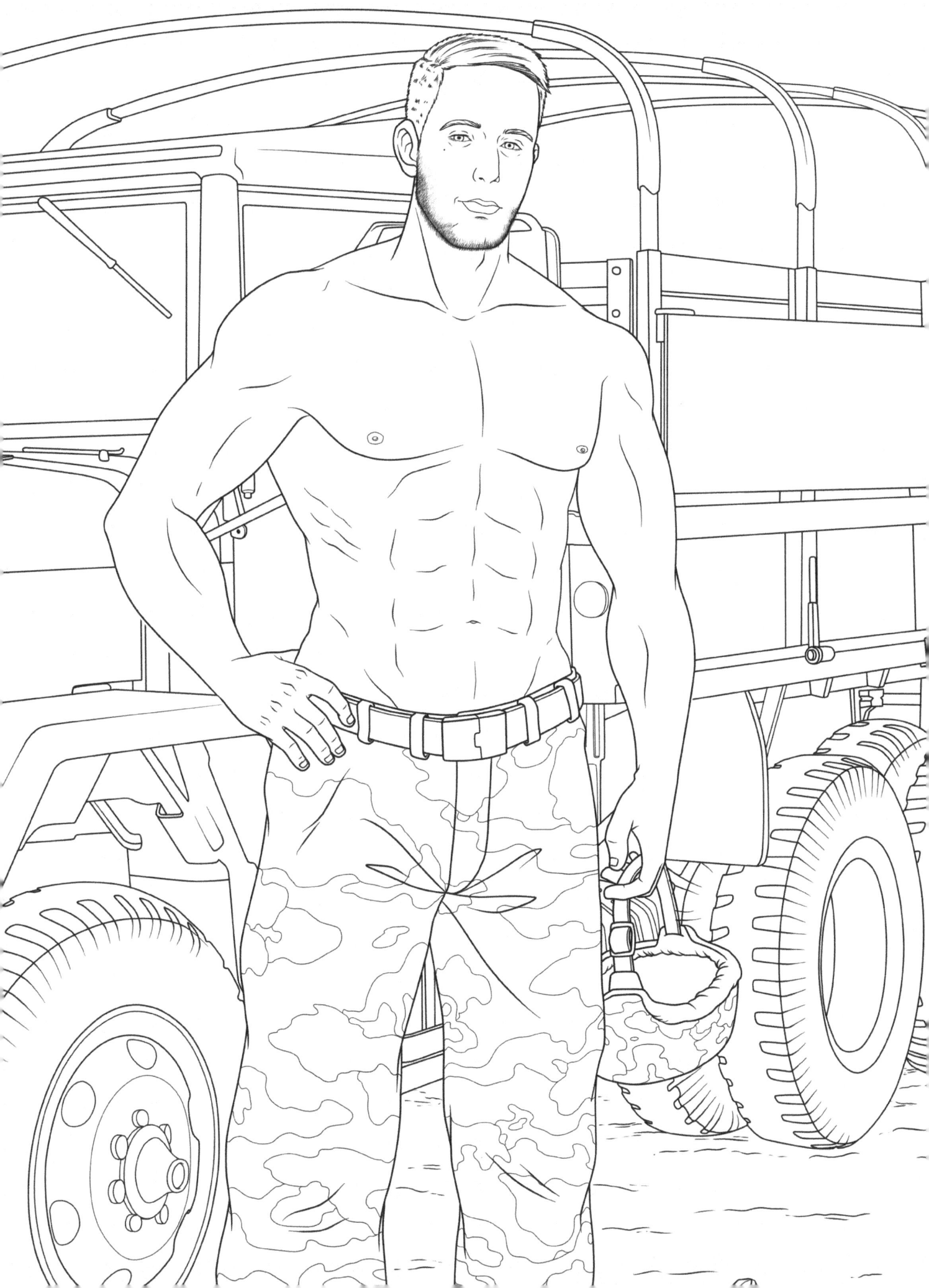

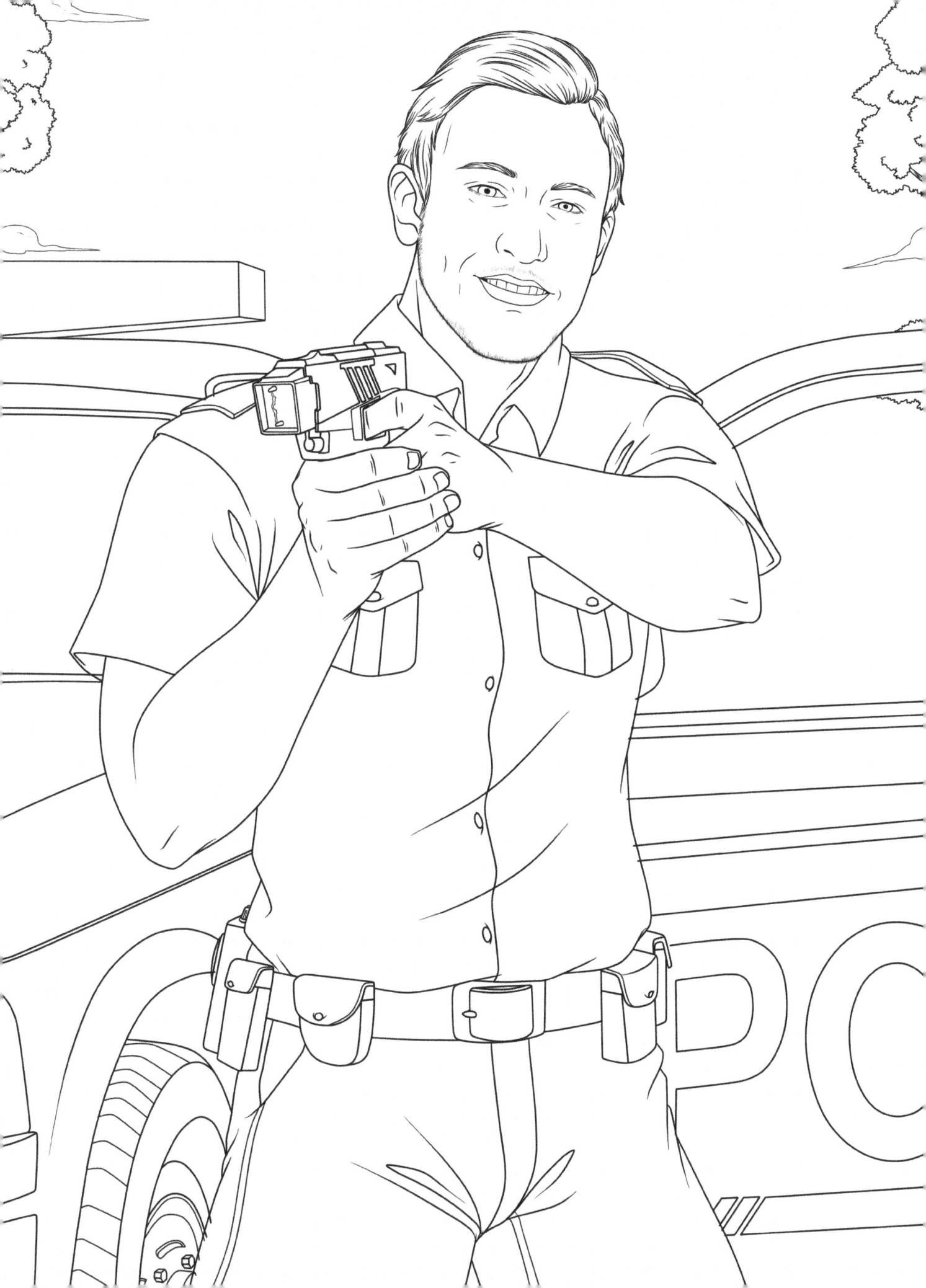

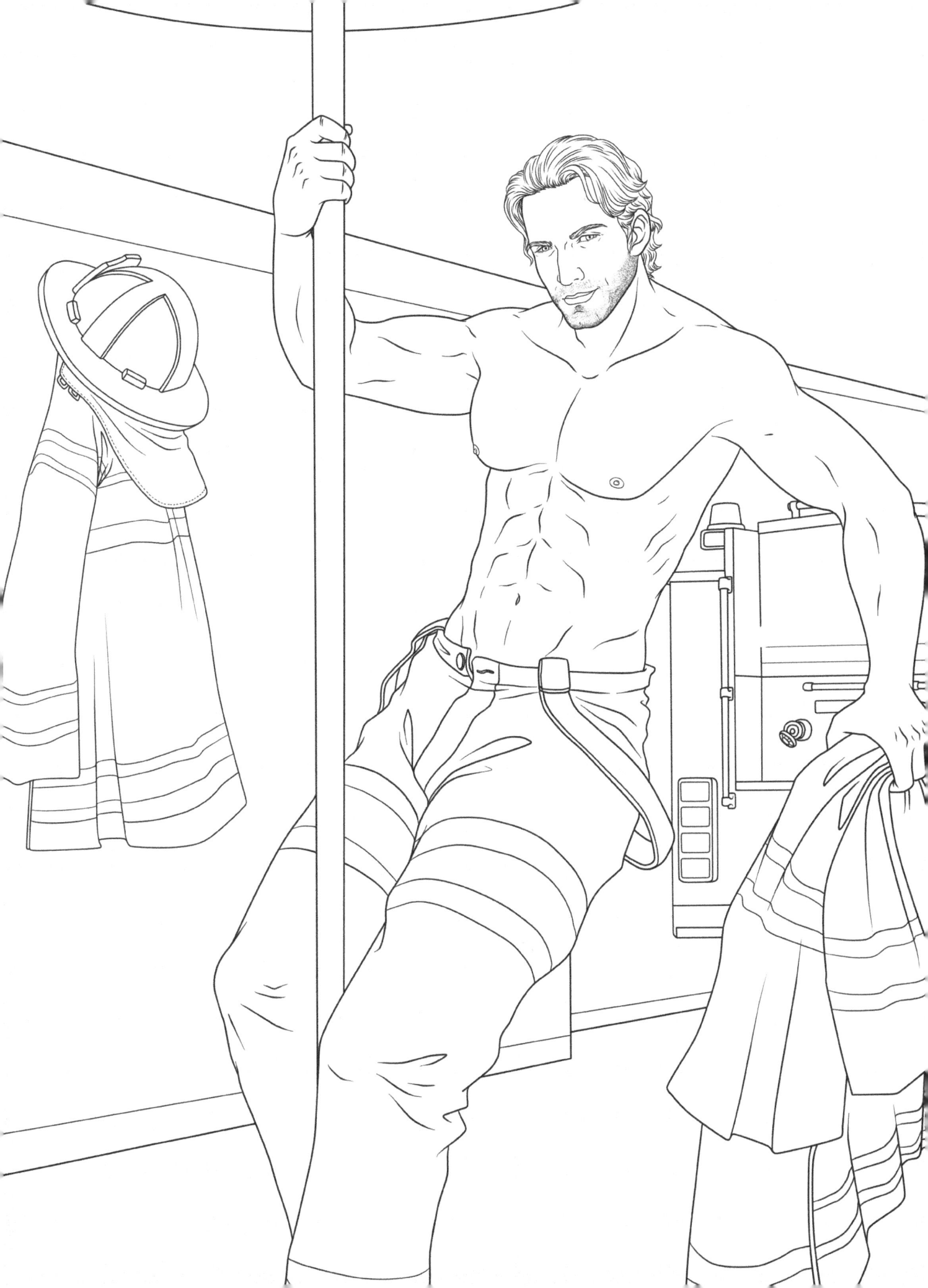

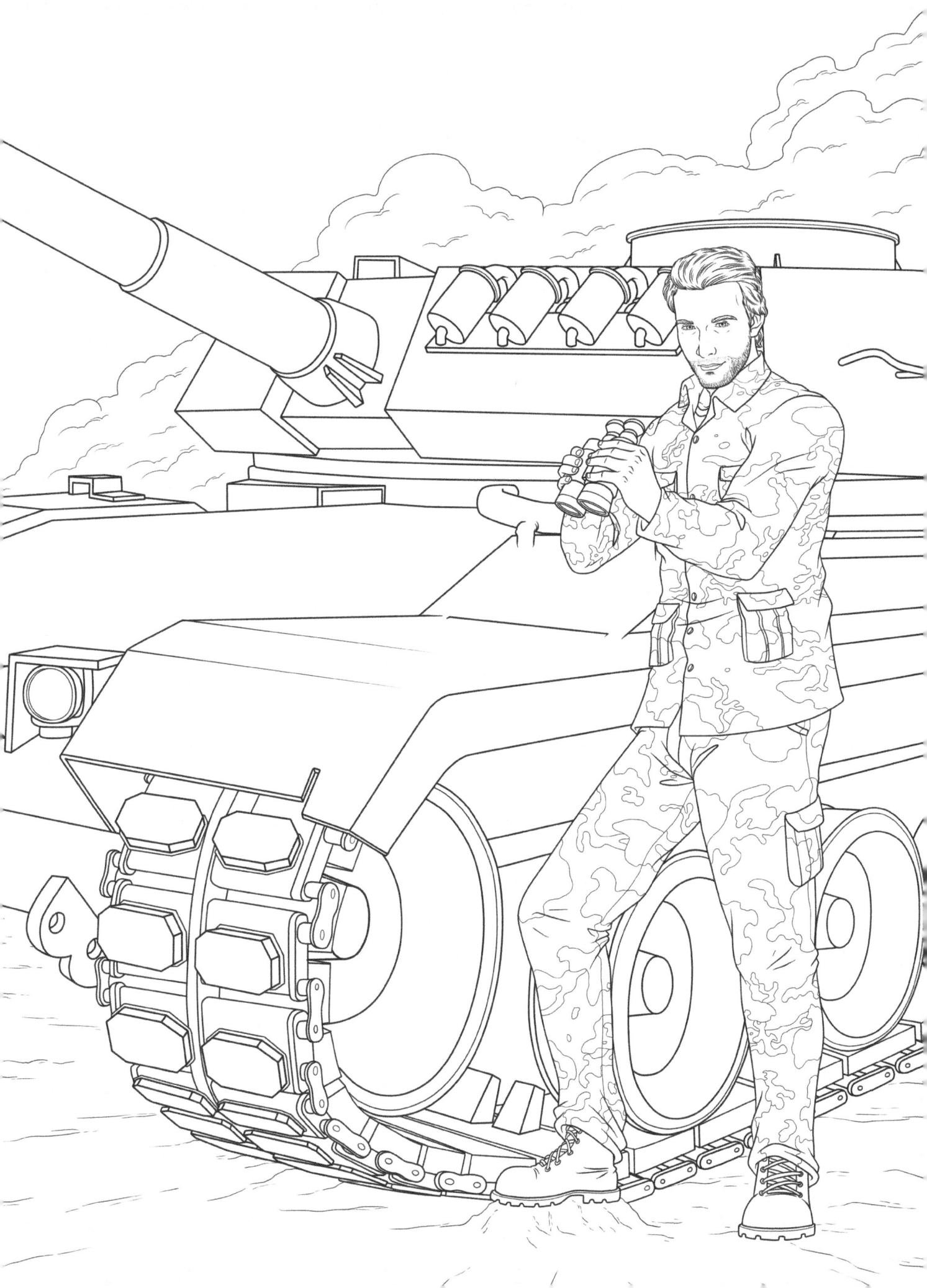

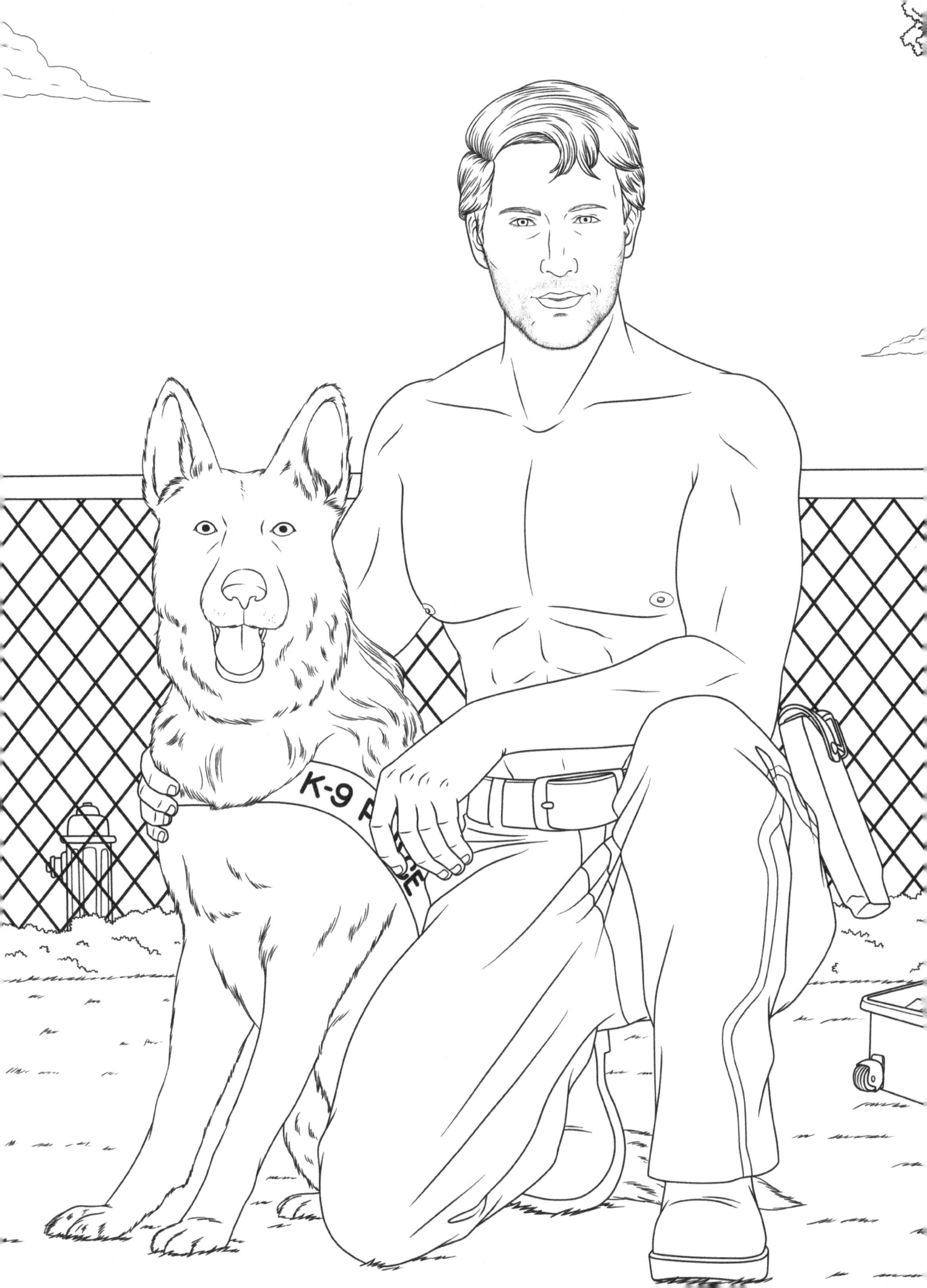
K-9

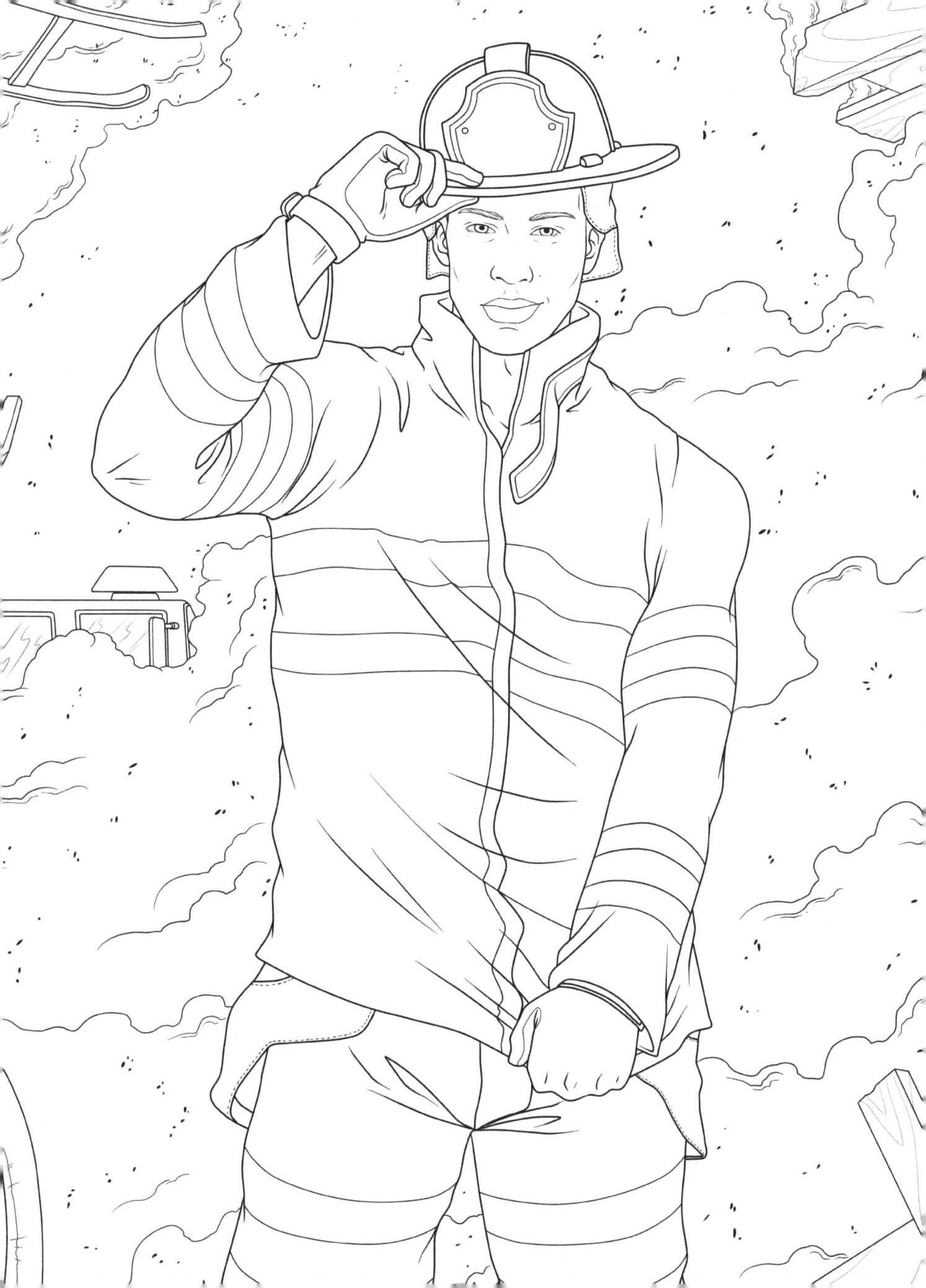

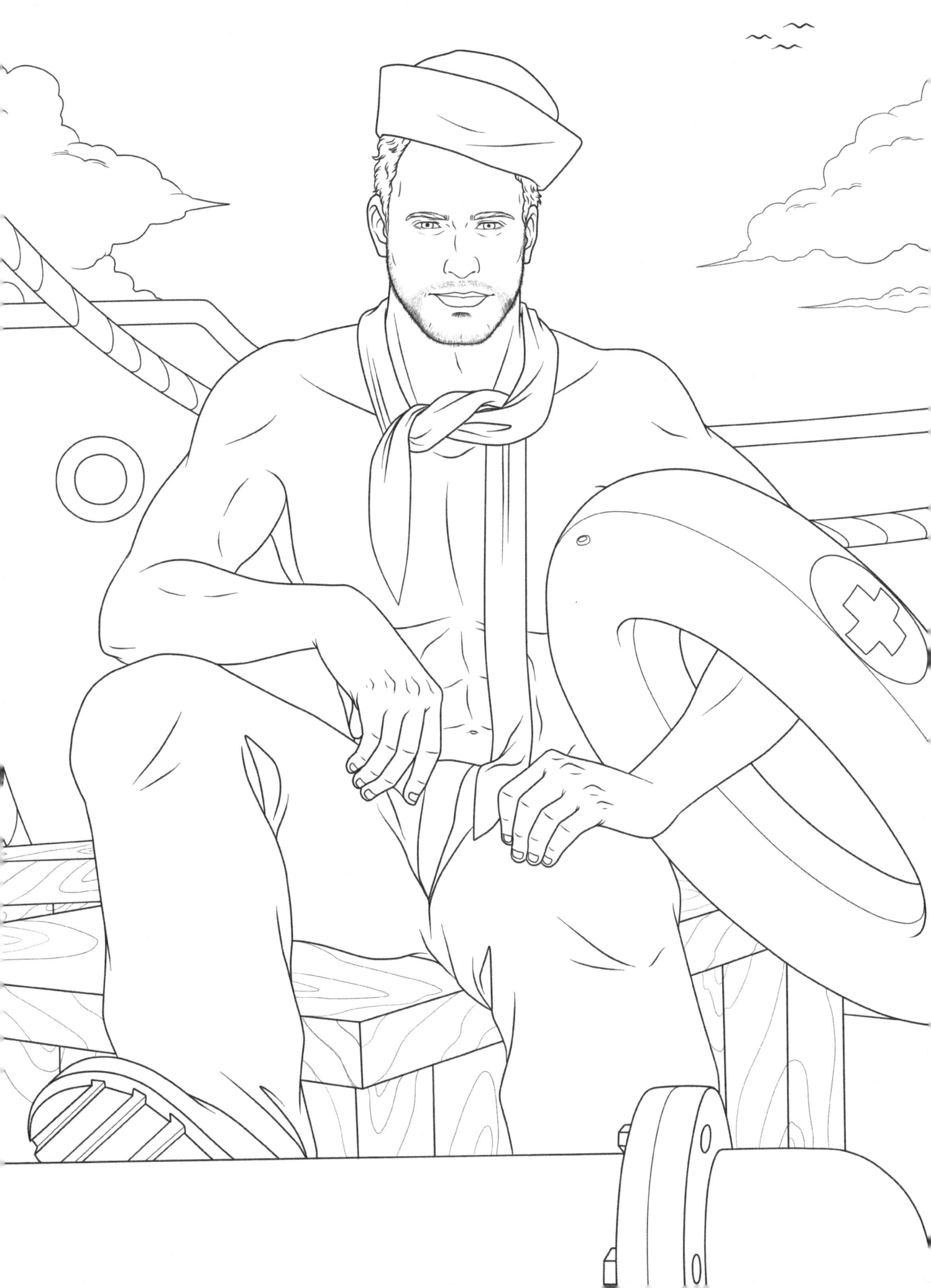

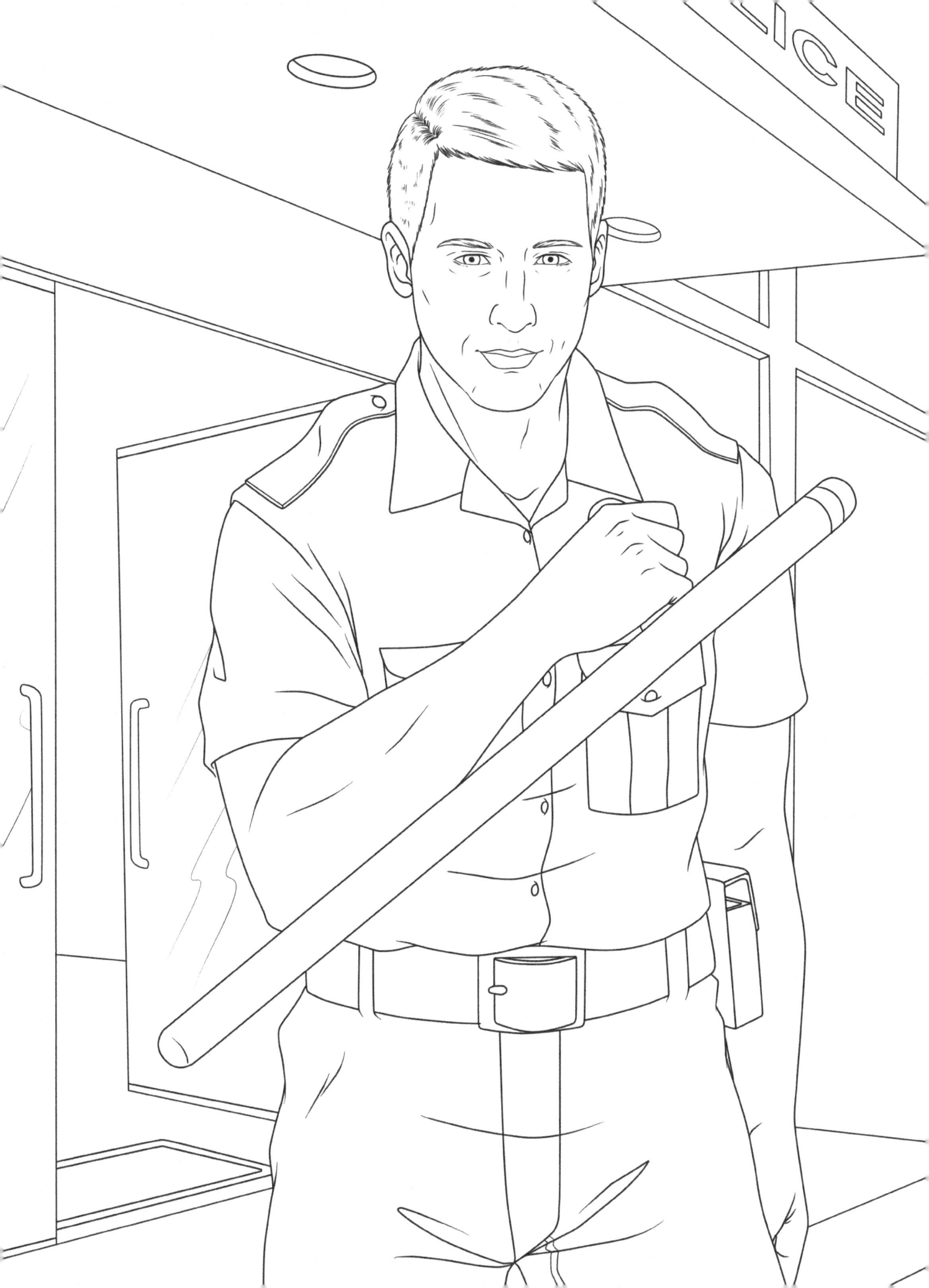
ICE

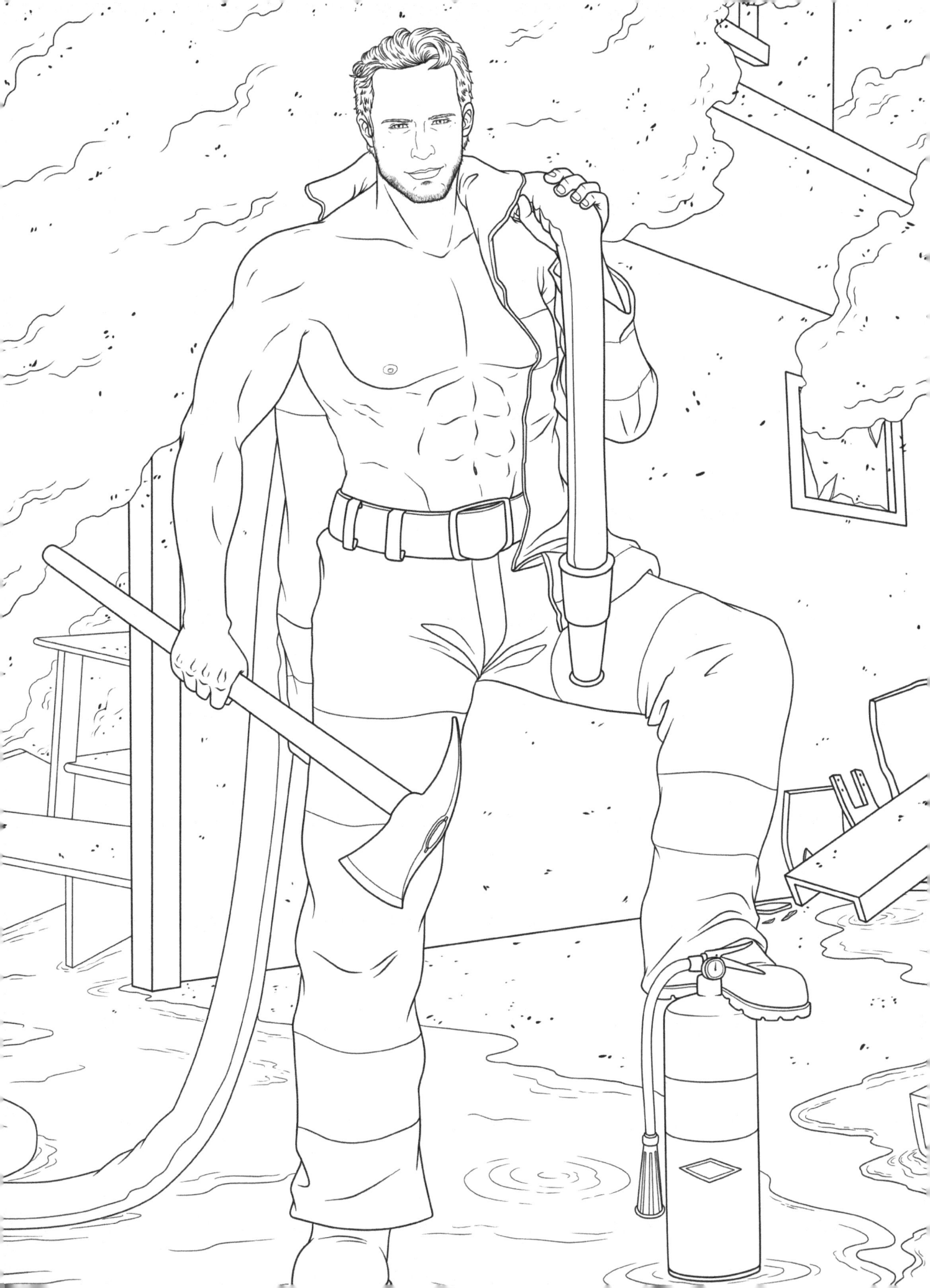

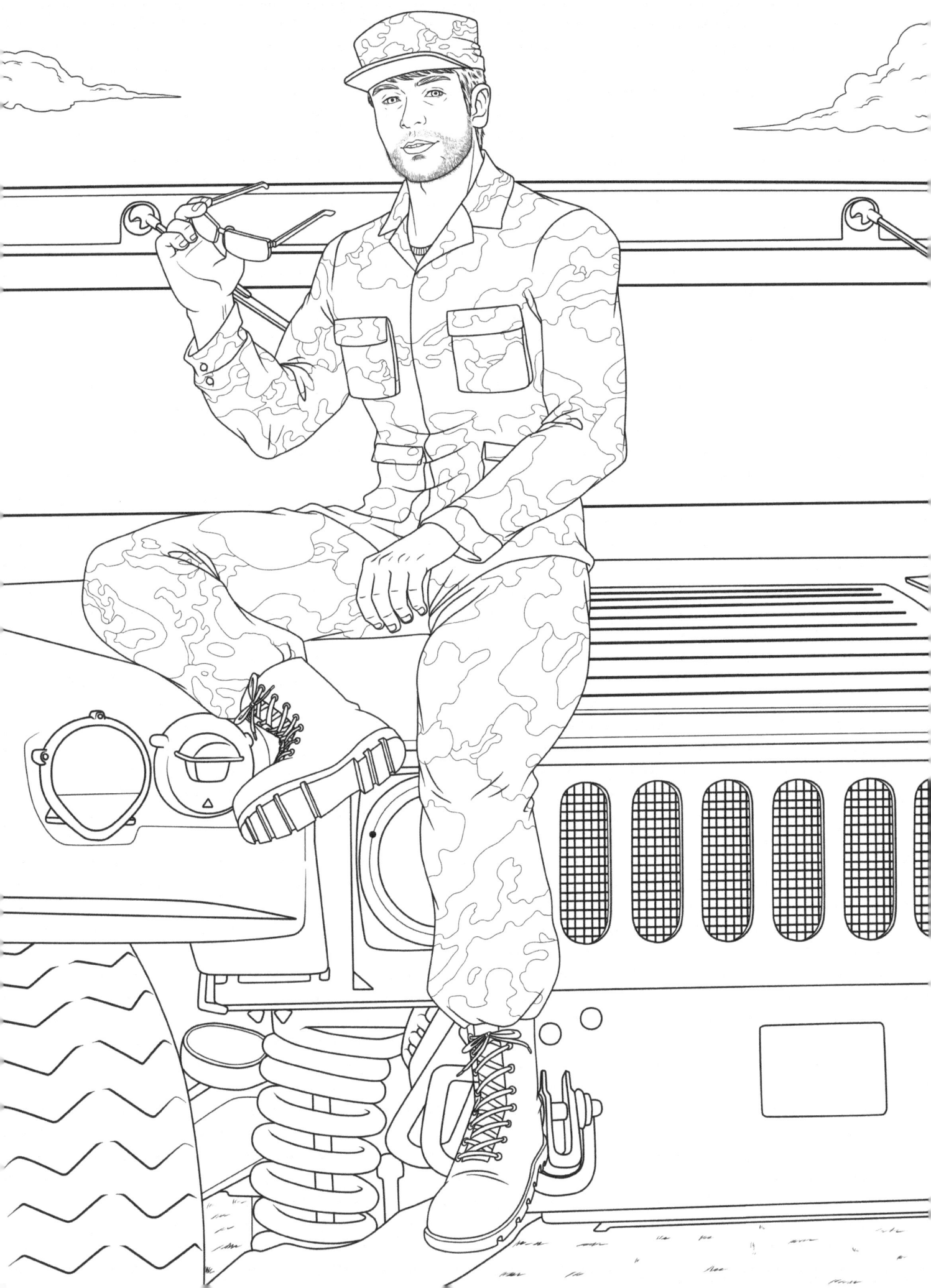

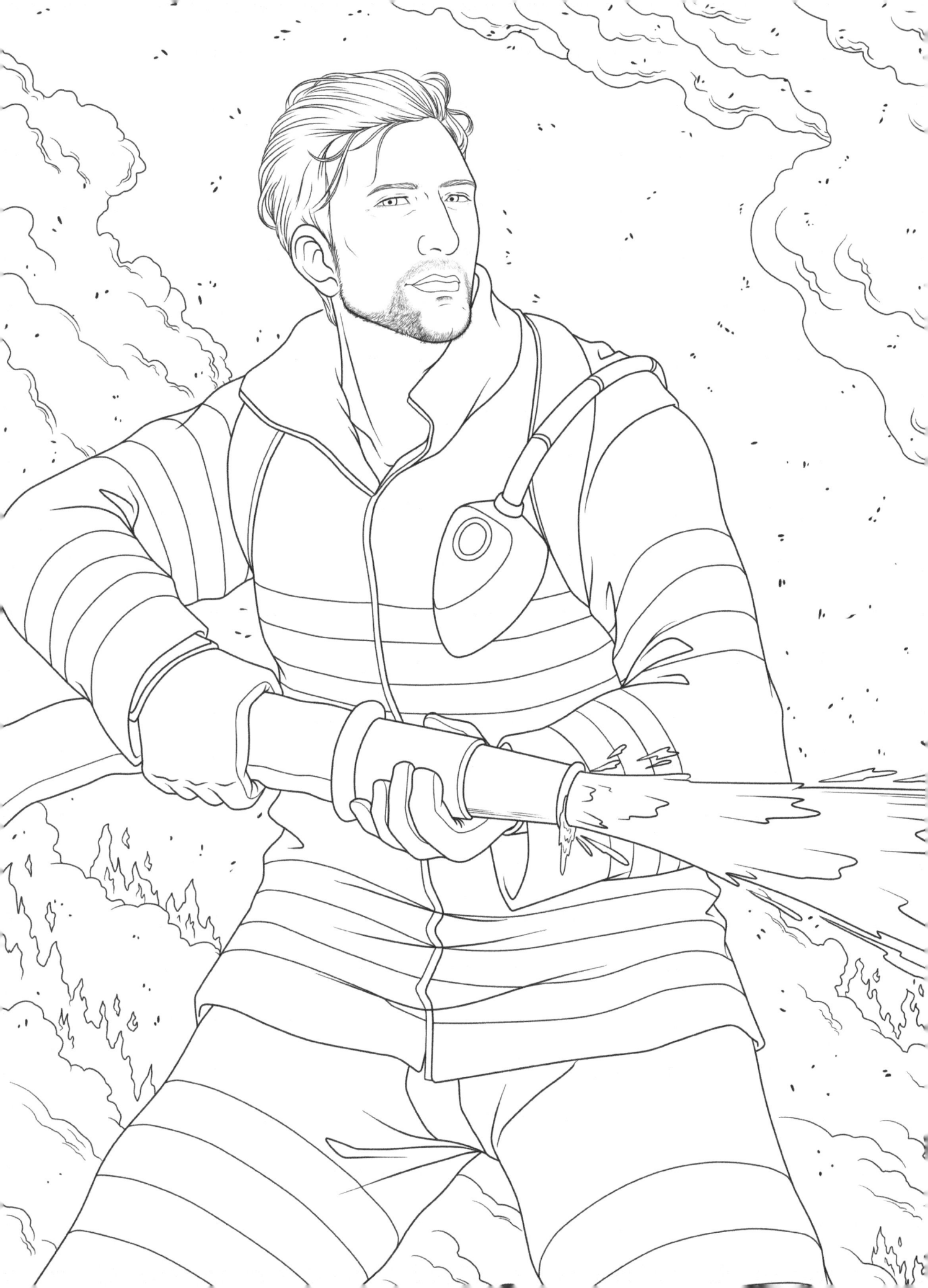

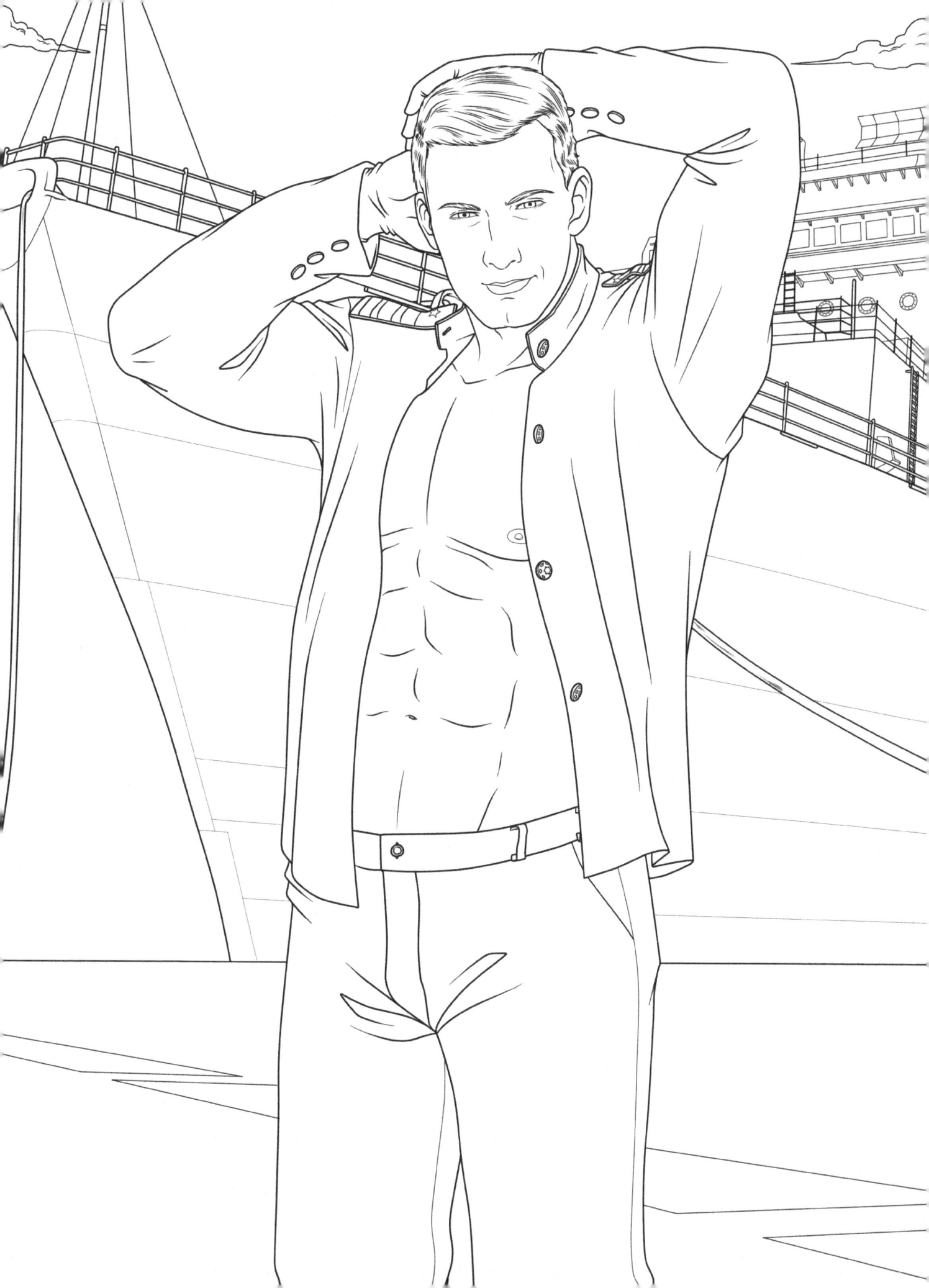

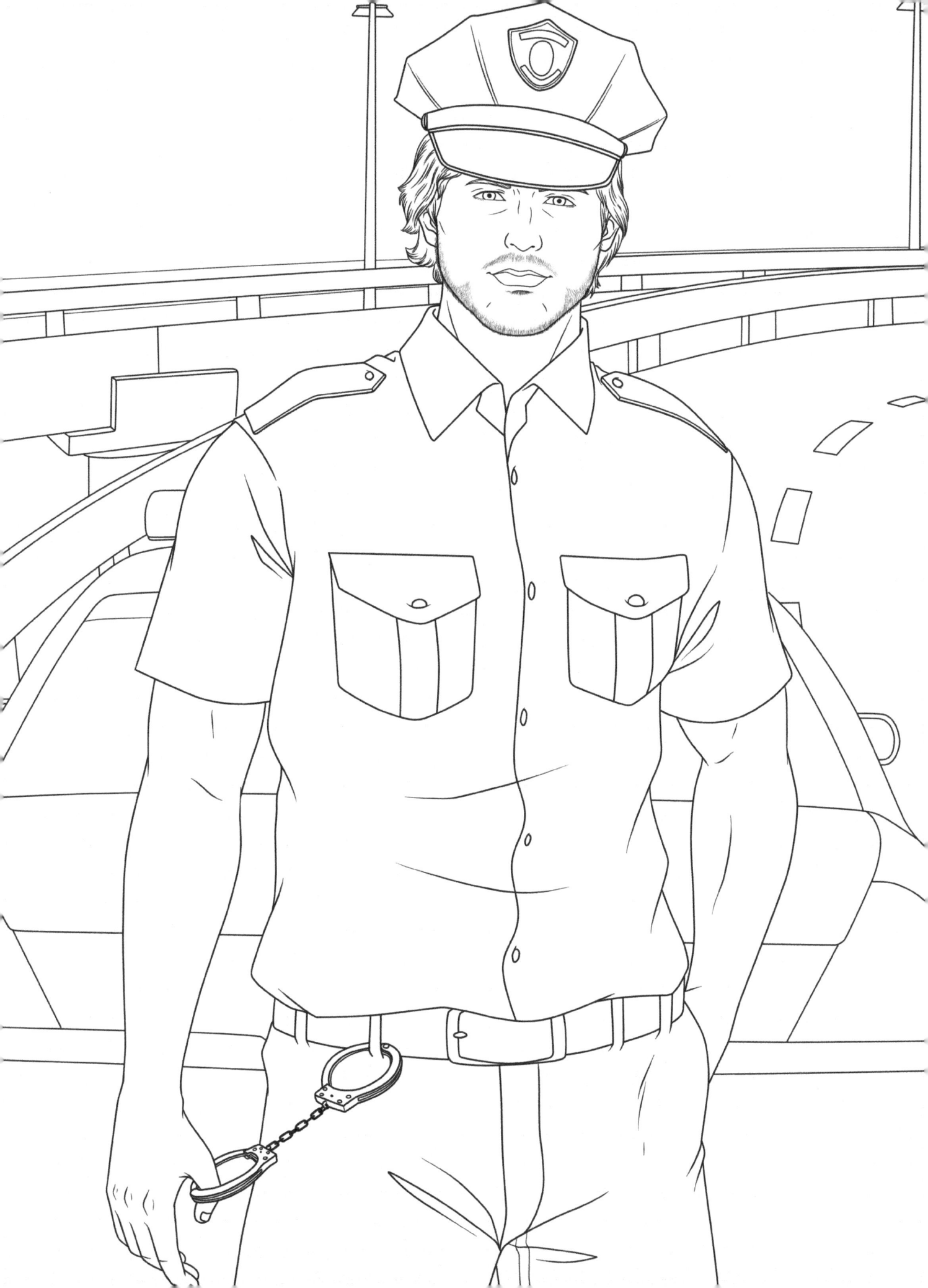

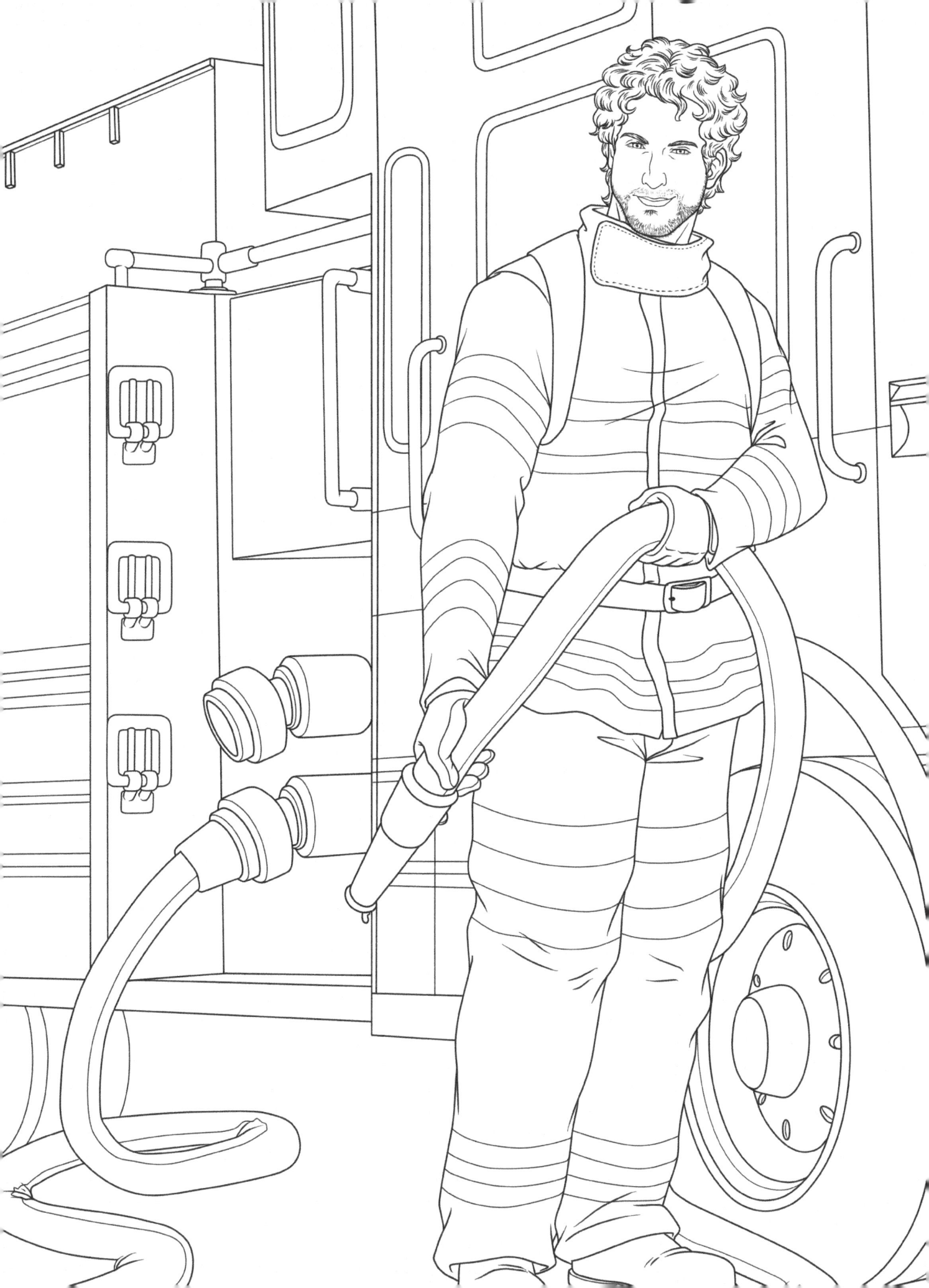

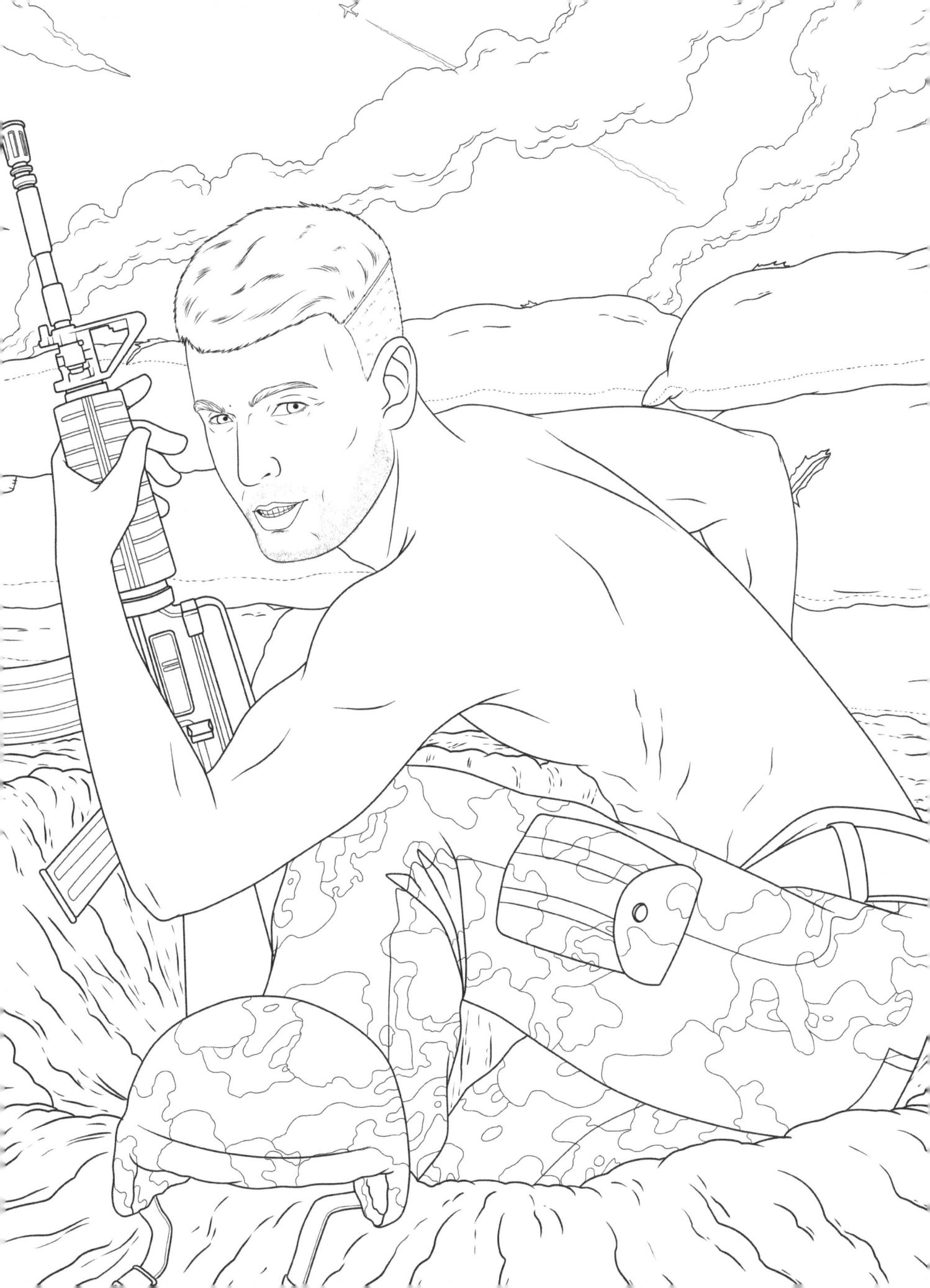

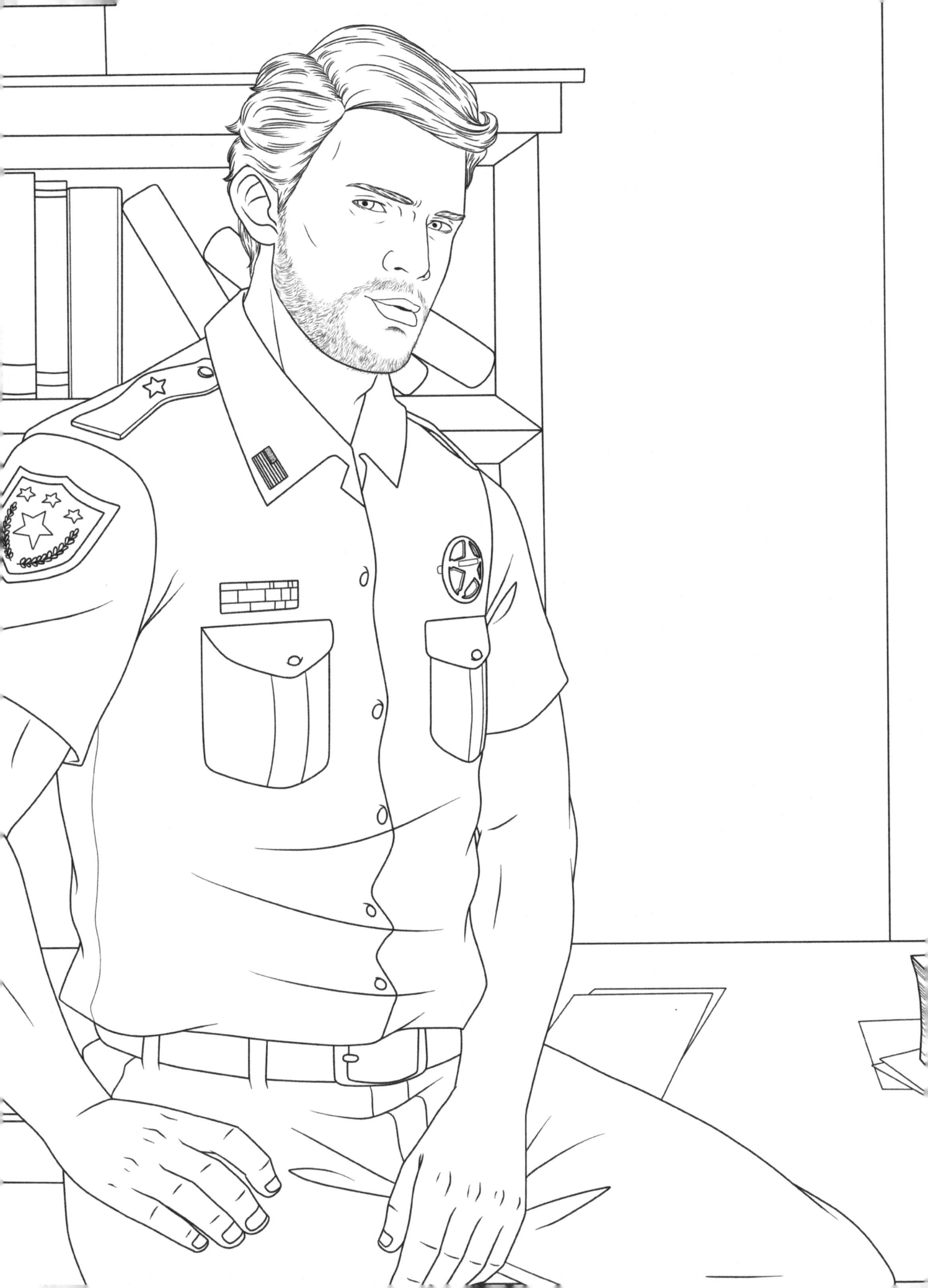

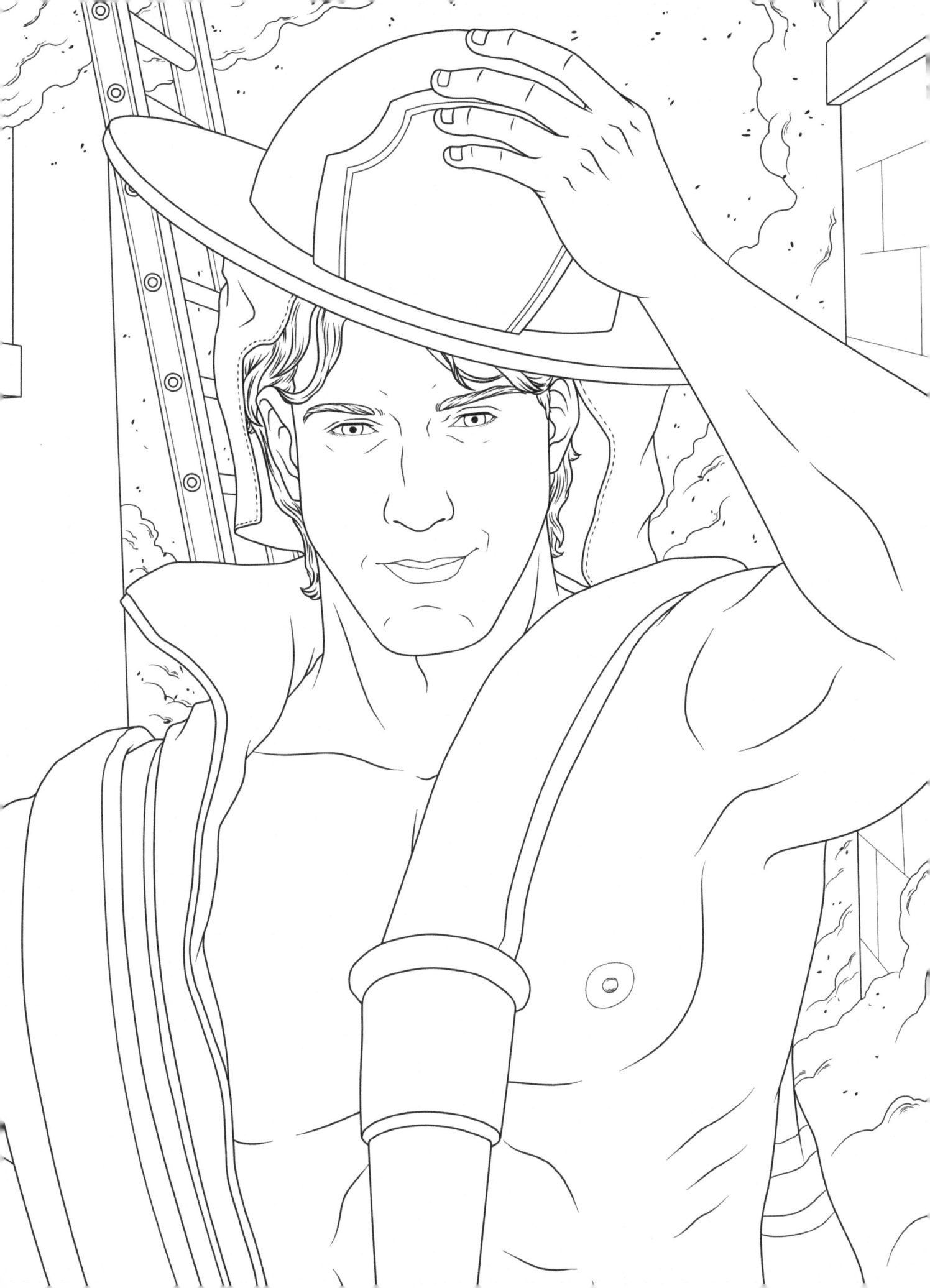

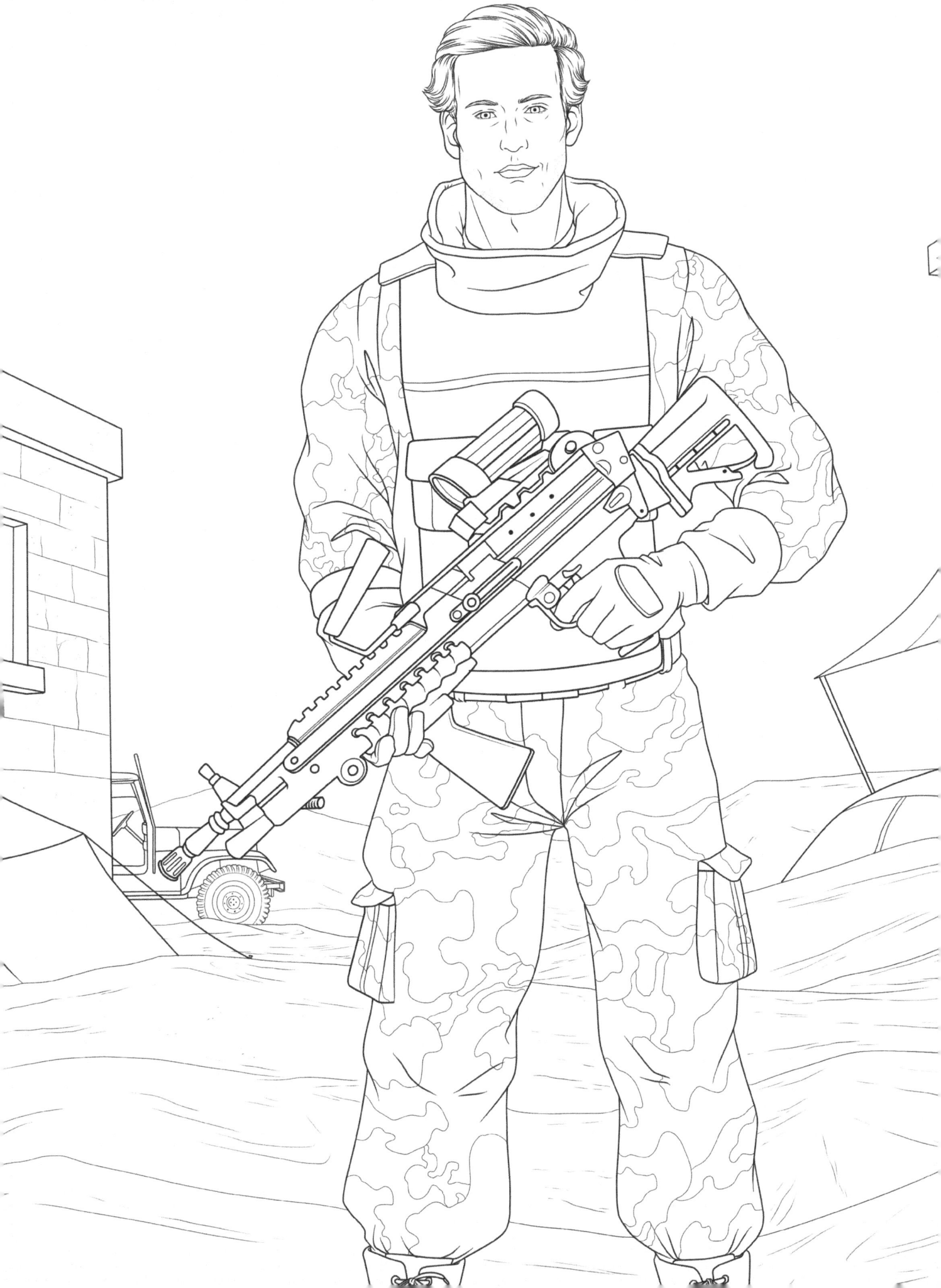